NEW
YORK

NEW YORK

Carole Chester

Cathay Books

CONTENTS

INTRODUCTION
6

FROM SKYSCRAPERS TO BROWNSTONES
8

NEW YORKERS
28

ENJOYING THE BIG APPLE
40

MAKING A BUCK
52

INDEX
64

First published in 1982 by Cathay Books
59 Grosvenor Street, London W1
© 1981 Hennerwood Publications Limited

ISBN 0 86178 161 9

Produced by Mandarin Publishers Limited
22a Westlands Road
Quarry Bay, Hong Kong

Printed in Hong Kong

INTRODUCTION

They call it 'The Big Apple' because everyone wants to take a bite. New York is a magnet for the rich and famous, and the down and out. Yesterday, people came from Ireland, Italy and Poland seeking a fortune. Some found it. Today's city is still a mass of ethnic quarters – Germantown, Chinatown, Little Italy, Harlem – whose heritage lingers on in shops and restaurants, attitudes and traditions.

The island purchased for a string of beads is not America's capital but it could well be, for Manhattan (an Indian name meaning 'a dangerous stream of running water') has grown into a giant port, meeting place and money mecca. It has given birth to the skyscraper, forming a world-famous skyline; created fashions and fads and introduced 'fast food' to the rest of the world. It boasts the world's largest department store and the second highest building. Its pioneers are remembered by city features. Henry Hudson, often wrongly considered to be the first European to arrive in the bay, has a river named after him, while an Italian, Giovanni da Verrazano, who was here in 1524, has a huge suspension bridge to his credit, a particularly well-designed one.

New York is mercurial. This year's trendy discothèque is tomorrow's hole in the ground. Its air is electric and its pace of life, excitingly fast. Yet there is tranquillity in its pocket parks, tiny squares of green, oases in cement canyons And there is culture and dignity in its magnificent museums and art galleries.

This place is the home of the cocktail – half price at 'Happy Hour' in almost any bar. A place where cops whistle at a pretty girl, where you can drink round the clock if you wish, buy an exotic plant at 2 am, or find a Viennese watchmaker. It is a town where the unexpected is expected: a jogging marathon, an impromptu rock concert in Central Park. A city of eccentricities and lovable characters like the cabbie who insists on telling you his life story. A place of parades: for Easter, for St Patrick's Day, for Christmas or simply for fun.

In New York, terraced houses are called brownstones and broken-down warehouses are cleverly converted into boutiques or restaurants. When it was New Amsterdam, under Dutch rule, it may have been staid but the New York City on view now is anything but.

Page 1 The World Trade Center's gleaming twin towers.

Pages 2 and 3 A view from a helicopter of the Battery and southern Manhattan.

Pages 4 and 5 Central Park's skating rink attracts people of all ages.

Left Whatever the gear – and accessories (even the live kind) – Central Park sees it all.

FROM SKYSCRAPERS TO BROWNSTONES

They stretch skywards, gleaming towers clothed in tinted glass and shiny chrome – New York's skyscrapers – the trademark of this city whose aerial view is one of the world's most magnificent. Each newly erected monolith is taller, more glossy than the last so that in just over eight decades what was once the world's highest edifice, Broadway's Woolworth Building, has been dwarfed many times by office blocks and hotels. In fact, one of the newest and most impressive, the twin-towered World Trade Center, has changed the skyline completely.

Architects have been dramatic and flamboyant with shape and line, creating showpieces and talking pieces like Frank Lloyd Wright's unusual Guggenheim Museum and Marcel Breuer's Whitney Museum which looks like an inverted layer cake.

Those once prevalent raised railways such as the notorious 'Third Ave. El' have disappeared below ground, but old world New York shows its face every now and then in quiet side streets – brownstones with exterior iron fire escapes and quaint churches dating from Manhattan's early days, like Trinity tucked into busy Wall Street.

Preservation orders ensure that Lower Manhattan's colonial and federal period homes still stand, like the handsome red brick mansions bordering Washington Square and Schemerhorn Row on Fulton and Front Streets.

Manhattan's skyline (preceding pages) is probably the world's most famous, especially when the camera catches it in some unusual light, but it has constantly changed. It was not always dominated by the two giant towers of the World Trade Center as it is now. That site used to be occupied by warehouses.

With so many people to cram into such a small space, the only way to expand was up, so it is not surprising that low buildings have often given way to the sledge-hammer. But there are still some architectural reminders of Manhattan's embryo days when the southern tip *was* New York and the rest of the island, countryside. Battery Park, for instance, even survived the building of the Battery Tunnel. Wouter van Twiller, who succeeded Peter Minuit (the original purchaser of Manhattan), built a fort here which later became the setting for a gala evening in honour of Lafayette and a concert by singer Jenny Lind. That reconstructed fort is today's Castle Clinton on this sea-breezy green esplanade.

Pier A, too, has been saved. Its Disneyesque green-roofed building is now a fire department but its clock still chimes ships' bells. And Bowling Green, where those Dutch burghers really did play bowls, has retained its name. On this patch of green in front of the massive neoclassic US Customs House, stand the statues of four continents, Asia, America, Europe and Africa. The fence around them is the original one the British put up but after 1776 the crown disappeared. Once upon a time, a statue of George III stood here as well but, as soon as the War of Independence started, angry colonists broke it up and scattered the pieces in Flushing (the borough of Queens). Well, the British are now back in favour – archaeologists have recently rediscovered some of those pieces and New York is thinking about putting George back.

From a terminal near Battery Park, passengers can take the ferry to Staten Island – one of the best bargains in town. Pear-shaped Staten Island is part of New York, home to many commuters and on the visitor's sightseeing itinerary to boot. Stop off there for a view of Bentley Manor House. It was at this residence that Benjamin Franklin proved to be not quite such a successful negotiator as everyone had thought. In 1776, Franklin, John Adams and Edward Rutledge, representing the continental congress, met with Lord Howe to discuss peace. They failed.

What is now Fort Wadsworth was a Dutch blockhouse which was overcome by the British when they sailed into New York harbour. And Snug Harbor, once the home of retired seamen, is now a haven for the arts. Its five handsome Greek revival-style buildings in a 32-hectare (80-acre) park setting have been designated city landmarks and are worth touring. Richmondtown, the former county seat of Staten Island, dates back to pre-revolution days and will one day be a historic showplace of importance.

On the way to Staten Island, Governor's Island and Ellis Island can be seen. Until 1954, the latter was gateway to America for shiploads of immigrants. But the sight they all waited to see, and the highlight of the 20-minute boat ride, is the **Statue of Liberty** (right) which houses an immigration museum in its base. New York's most celebrated lady was a gift from the French in 1886 to commemorate the alliance of the two countries during the War of Independence. Its sculptor, Frédéric Auguste Bartholdi, raised funds in France for his monumental design without very much difficulty, but the Americans at the time were reluctant to match France's one million-franc contribution. It was left to Joseph Pulitzer, editor of the *New York World*, to coax them with an intensive newspaper campaign.

The money was eventually found and Liberty looks so right in Upper Bay. As she steps from her chains, she is an ideal symbol for America, an especially welcome sight for the millions of immigrants seeking a new life in this new world. In her left hand, Liberty holds a tablet of the Declaration of Independence and in her right, high above her head, the torch of freedom. When viewed from the ferry, her height is misleading. Up close one realizes that raising the statue was quite a feat. (It was, in fact, accomplished with the aid of Alexandre Gustave Eiffel's supporting framework.) The pedestal alone stands 45·7 metres (150 feet) high and a lift takes visitors to the top of this. But the figure itself is another 46·3 metres (152 feet) high which means 12 floors of stairs to be climbed before reaching the observation room inside the statue's crown.

Liberty Island was bought by the State of New York in 1796 and was ceded to the Federal government in 1880. Before 1796, the island was owned by and named after the Bedloe family.

From the bay, Manhattan looks particularly spectacular at night, lit up and glittering, but it is almost equally magnificent when viewed from across the **Brooklyn Bridge** (overleaf).

Brooklyn Bridge (left) is both a splendid feat of engineering and rather attractive to look at. It is the achievement of John Roebling and his son, Washington, and took 13 years to build, being completed in 1883. Its majestic Italian Renaissance-style granite bridge towers are in sharp contrast to the open tapestry of its cables. Until 1903 the Brooklyn Bridge claimed the title of being the world's longest suspension bridge.

Subsequently, other bridges took on the title – none more important than the Verrazano-Narrows which links Staten Island with Brooklyn. Named after the Italian explorer, Giovanni da Verrazano, who first sighted Staten Island in 1524, this bridge arching across the Narrows is today's longest suspension type (until Britain's Humber opens) with a staggering span of 1,298 metres (4,260 feet). That's 18 metres (60 feet) longer than San Francisco's Golden Gate!

Unless you happen to be in the panoramic cocktail lounge of the World Trade Center, the best unobstructed view of Brooklyn Bridge (from the Manhattan side) is from the end of Pier 16 at the foot of Fulton Street.

The bridge entrance lies opposite another of New York's architectural gems – City Hall, a fine example of the Federal period and considered by many to be one of America's most beautiful buildings. Situated at Broadway and Murray Streets, it has been the seat of New York's municipal government since it opened in 1812. Architects Joseph Mangin, a refugee from France's Reign of Terror, and John McComb Jr, the Scottish designer of Castle Clinton, have combined a Georgian form with French Renaissance detail. Inside, the central domed space contains twin spiral marble staircases, not surprisingly exactly the right setting for state funerals. Several were held here including those of Presidents Grant and Lincoln. Visitors can see the Governor's Room, too, which contains a notable collection of historic portraits and antique furniture including two writing tables used by George Washington.

During the Dutch period, adjacent City Hall Park was first a pasture and then a parade ground. It was here that the Declaration of Independence was read before Washington and his troops on 9 July 1776.

George Washington is closely associated with many buildings in Lower Manhattan, especially **Fraunces Tavern** (above right) at 54 Pearl Street where he frequently dined. This fine neo-Georgian brick structure was initially the 1719 residence of Etienne de Lancey, a Huguenot born in France, who often entertained with his wife, Anne (from the eminent van Cortlandt family). It has been the location of many governmental meetings and has hosted numerous politicians both then and later when it became a tavern. Samuel Fraunces, a West Indian, took over proprietorship in 1762 and it went down in history when George Washington bade farewell to his troops in its Long Room in 1783. That same room is still furnished in 18th-century style and the rest of the museum's exhibits reflect other parts of New York's early history. Today the Tavern lies at the end of one of the few remaining complete blocks of 18th- and 19th-century buildings. Like much of Lower Manhattan, the block was built on reclaimed land as the shoreline in Dutch times was along Pearl Street.

During his presidency, George Washington worshipped at St Paul's Chapel. It's Manhattan's oldest surviving church, even older than Trinity itself. Said to have been inspired by St Martin-in-the-Fields in London, St Paul's was finished in 1766 but the tower and steeple were not added until 1794. It has always had a distinguished patronage: during British rule, the royal governor of the province of New York was a frequent worshipper. Lafayette, Lords Cornwallis and Howe and many a US president have also prayed here. A number of original artifacts adorn the church today.

While on the subject of churches, not far away is another worth looking at – Old John Street Methodist Church. Although the present building was erected here in 1841, America's first methodist church was built on the same site in 1768, and her first commercial telephone (British made) was installed in the cellar of St John's Church!

The best way to take advantage of what Lower Manhattan has to offer is to walk around it. History buffs with an eye for detail will find plenty to fascinate them. Who would know, for example, that the world's largest digital clock is on the east wall of 127 John Street? And who would realize that the Continental Insurance Company has a historic home – until you look at the ornamental cast iron façade at 90 Maiden Lane.

In the past, cast iron was used a great deal for decoration because it could achieve the same effects as

COMPANY

RENE BLOCK
GAL ERY

409

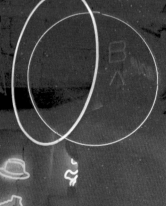

MATTRESSES
MADE OVER

stone at a much lower cost. The main district for cast
iron buildings has only fairly recently become New
York's trendiest area – SoHo. Not long ago, the region
bordered by West Broadway, Canal, Lafayette and
Houston consisted of dirty, derelict warehouses. Then
someone coined the name 'SoHo' – which stands for
south of Houston (Street) – and transformation was on its
way. Many of the rundown drab buildings in **SoHo** (left)
have taken on a very different look (inset left).
Commercial outlets have been supplanted by wildly
decorated bars and discothèques, unusually named
cafés and restaurants, plus a burgeoning number of
fashionable boutiques. We can thank the artists for
putting SoHo on the Manhattan map for, when
Greenwich Village (their former territory) became too
overcrowded and touristy, the serious painters moved
south into SoHo's lofts. One can now visit a number of
chic art galleries in the area's ground level and upper
studios or simply turn up for a fun evening on the town.

SoHo may have taken over where Greenwich Village
left off but that is not to say the latter is without its own
charm. Unlike most of the rest of the island, the Village
is not laid out in a grid system. Instead, this maze of
streets on the lower west side of Manhattan twist and
turn and are often flanked by beautiful **brownstones**
(above). Brownstones, which are three- or four-storey
terraced houses, are scattered throughout the city and
are highly sought after by well-heeled young families
and career types intent on renovation, when they have
not already been snapped up by the rich.

In Greenwich Village you can watch up-and-coming
talent perform in off-Broadway productions in tiny

theatres, play backgammon or chess in a coffee house
where there's sawdust on the floor, or have your portrait
painted on the spot. Jazz clubs, gay clubs, strip clubs –
the Village has them all, for the offbeat and the arts have
always been its big attraction.

In the 1920s when 'Bohemian' and 'avant garde' were
the terms used to describe the unconventional,
MacDougal Street was a free-thinkers' haven. Number
137 is the site of the old Liberal Club where birth
control was first preached. Next door, the Provincetown Playhouse had discovered a promising new
playwright by the name of Eugene O'Neill and an
equally talented young actess called Edna St Vincent
Millay, who lived at 75½ Bedford Street, still known as
the narrowest house in the village. Writers could afford
to be daring in the Village and, indeed, still are.
Fledgling talents anxious to be seen or heard have
created off-off-Broadway productions, often in
makeshift theatres, or those converted from churches or
old cellars and audience participation is quite often
expected!

One of the main streets for entertainment is Bleecker
and for shopping, Greenwich Avenue and West 4th. But
an amble through Washington Square Park dominated
by Stanford White's handsome Arch is well worth while
and is easy to find at Fifth Avenue and 8th Street. The
Greek Revival houses on its northern border are some
of the most elegant in New York. Novelist Henry James
used them as a setting for his *Washington Square*.
Originally, when this region was a genuine village,
quite separate from the city of New York in Lower
Manhattan, the ground here was marshland.

King Kong didn't exactly make the **Empire State Building** (preceding pages, left) famous but the film about Fay Wray's exploits with the Big Ape certainly made this celebrated skyscraper as familiar as London's Houses of Parliament.

Until the World Trade Center was built, the Empire State was Manhattan's tallest monolith at 449 metres (1,472 feet), with 102 floors. It may have relinquished that title but it continues to preside impressively over midtown Manhattan from its position on Fifth Avenue and 34th Street. Erected in 1931, it boasts two observatories – an open air one on the 86th floor and an enclosed one on the 102nd. From the outside promenade deck on the 86th, there is an all-round view and on a clear day it is possible to see as far as 80 km (50 miles). That view will reveal some of New York's other boroughs: across the Queensborough (59th Street) Bridge to Queens, home of Shea Stadium, where baseball is played, and the excellent Aqueduct and Belmont race tracks. (The Aqueduct with its seating capacity of 80,000 is America's largest of its kind, with its own subway stop.) Also in Queens is Forest Hills where international tennis is played. Look north to the Bronx, the only borough attached to the mainland and famous for its zoo and botanical garden, its parks and beaches. And look beyond New Jersey's cliffs on the other side of the Hudson. Looking down into the concrete canyons below, those fleets of yellow taxis

look no bigger than matchbox toys, and the people merely moving dots.

If observation roofs seem two a penny in New York it is only because the panoramic views from a height are so splendid by day or night. A glowing **midtown Manhattan** (previous pages, right) is visible from a lofty perch on top of an office building like the RCA, or from a comfortable cocktail lounge such as Top of the Sixes at 666 Fifth Avenue.

The RCA Building plus 20 other sleek skyscrapers are all part of the 9-hectare (22-acre) Rockefeller business and entertainment complex. It is one of New York's architectural marvels even if some 200 old houses had to be demolished to achieve the project. At the turn of the 18th century, a botanical garden and hothouse were constructed on the midtown site for research purposes, but by the mid-19th century the area had become residential. Around this time, the idea was to build an opera house here for which the late John D. Rockefeller took a lease in 1928. The opera house was never built but the complex was—1,400 businesses, 200-plus shops in underground arcades, restaurants, subway stop and parking garages!

Initially, the centre only took up 6 hectares (15 acres) between 48th and 51st Streets and Fifth and Sixth Avenues but it just grew and grew. For the best vantage point, it should be approached from the Channel Gardens, across Fifth Avenue from St Patrick's Cathedral, between 49th and 50th Streets. Floral displays change seasonally, adding much appreciated bright spots of colour, and office workers often prefer to grab a bite of lunch in the open air here rather than sit in a restaurant. A walk down the promenade leads to the focal point of the complex – the **Lower Plaza** (below left) which in summer is an open air café and in winter, a skating rink. The massive gilded statue of Prometheus is by Paul Manship with a fountain at the back of it and behind that, the 70-storey RCA Building. Underground concourses link all the offices so that no one has to suffer from bad weather or lack of air conditioning. Guided tours around the whole development take about an hour and include a look behind the scenes at Radio City Music Hall plus a stop at the Observation Roof. Drop in to McGraw Hill Building on Sixth Avenue at 49th Street to take in 'The New York Experience'. Real fog, blackouts, bubbles and a few other suprises are part of this multi-screen presentation of New York City's past and present.

There is no other office and shopping complex like the Rockefeller Center, but on the other hand it is not the only one. Across town at Lexington Avenue and 54th Street is one of Manhattan's newest skyscrapers, Citicorp Center, distinguished by its unique slanted roof. They say it is the world's eighth tallest building, at least until another new one comes along. This is the place for visitors who feel homesick for Europe as the triple-level international marketplace sells a number of familiar products and foods.

Landmarks do tend to come and go just like the tallest building titles, but one which has remained can be seen further down Lexington Avenue at 42nd Street. The **Chrysler Building** (right) is a much-loved example of 1930s' art deco architecture. Its unusual decorative spire has kept it in favour with New Yorkers – and oh yes, it was tallest building for all of one year!

The general opinion about the Pan Am Building is that it spoils **Park Avenue** (left) but there is no doubt it is a landmark and that the avenue it overlooks is one of New York's loveliest. Park Avenue is more like a Continental boulevard than any other. Although, of course, commercial concerns do flank it, upper Park Avenue is very residential and any address here is a prestigious one. Below the Pan Am Building is known as Park Avenue South. What makes the skyscraper unique is that it sits on top of Grand Central Station which is both an outstanding work of engineering and a piece of renaissance-style architecture. The terminal has two levels of tracks accommodating a daily volume of more than 550 trains. Its main concourse is one of the largest rooms in the world.

A far more popular skyscraper (and yet another landmark) is the Seagram Building between 52nd and 53rd Streets. A gleaming bronze tower designed by Philip Johnson and Mies van der Rohe, it is considered by many to be one of the city's finest. New Yorkers loll in the surrounding grounds which have trees and fountains, while anyone with a fat wallet should dine, or at least sip a cocktail or two, in the Four Seasons Restaurant in the Seagram Building. It is one of Manhattan's showplace eating spots with its Picasso mural and its Pool Room which features a bubbling marble pool in the centre. Park Avenue is not without chic hotels either. The top name has to be the Waldorf Astoria if only because there can't be anyone who hasn't heard of it. The original Waldorf actually stood on the site of the Empire State, but the present hotel on 50th Street and Park has hosted many of the world's most

celebrated people including names like Bob Hope and the Duchess of Windsor.

One of New York's most noteworthy synagogues is located on Park Avenue, too, at 87th Street. The adjacent Milton Steinberg Building, named after its late renowned rabbi, has the largest continuous stained glass façade in the world. Designed by Adolph Gottlieb, it consists of 91 individual panes and portrays religious holidays and traditions. Free industrial exhibits are also an interesting aspect of New York. Lever House, on Park at 54th Street, is constantly changing its lobby displays while Union Carbide Building's exhibition hall on 47th Street is well worth looking at. (There are similar exhibitions, by the way, in other corporate buildings around town, most notably Burlington Industries 'The Mill' and Eastman Kodak's photo centre – both on Sixth Avenue – plus Allied Chemicals Exhibit Centre at Times Square.)

A few blocks east of the Pan Am Building is a sight that shouldn't be missed – **United Nations Building** (above). This international enclave is headquarters for several thousand foreigners who carry on the work of the Secretariat and the General Assembly. Member nations have donated several pieces of sculpture and works of art like the massive statue in the garden of a Soviet worker beating a sword into a plowshare. There are guided tours of the UN and visitors can attend one of the General Assembly or other meetings. Tickets are issued in the lobby on a first come first served basis, just before the meetings start. Once inside earphones are available, so it is possible to listen to the debates, some of which can be very lively.

New York has so many treasure houses in the form of museums and art galleries that the visitor with little time has to be selective and disciplined about which to visit. The **Guggenheim** (above) is a must. Not everyone admires Frank Lloyd Wright's design, but it is certainly a talking point. The building consists of a large circular ramp on which hang Solomon Guggenheim's collection of abstract, avant garde and generally way-out paintings. An 'old master' here, for example, is likely to be a Chagall or a Picasso!

The Museum of Modern Art, too, has been equally controversial since it opened in 1939 on West 53rd Street. At the time, its daring exhibits, like fur-lined teacups and Cubist pictures, shocked the rather staid art world. Once again, the emphasis is on 20th-century painters, like Mondrian and Braque. Take a look at the outdoor sculpture garden and perhaps catch a Garbo classic in the downstairs cinema which only features old films. Another modern building worth more than a second glance is Marcel Breuer's Whitney Museum on Madison Avenue at 75th Street. The outside is reminiscent of an inverted layer cake but inside there is a superb collection of contemporary art. Like the Museum of Modern Art, it, too, boasts an outside sculpture garden. Not every museum is quite so unconventional. The Metropolitan Museum of Art on Fifth Avenue at 82nd Street is the grand dowager of the city's museums and one of the world's most important. Whether you are interested in Egyptian artifacts, Roman armour, Chinese porcelain, Renaissance or Impressionist paintings, this is the place. The American Wing makes a good follow-up to a tour of Lower Manhattan as it has reconstructed rooms from the Colonial, Revolutionary and Republican periods. Lectures and film shows are often given at the museum and taking tea is a treat in the Met's poolside restaurant.

One of Manhattan's most imaginative small museums is the Contemporary Crafts on West 53rd Street. And a much-loved little gem is the Frick Collection on East 70th Street. This beautiful little Fifth Avenue mansion was formerly the home of steel magnate, Henry Clay Frick. The setting is perfect for the free concerts sometimes held there.

When it comes to landmark churches, **St Patrick's Cathedral** (right), on Fifth Avenue at 50th Street, has to top the list. Pictured here reflected in the glassed exterior of the Olympic-Onassis Building, it is one of New York's most traditional, best-known and most-loved churches. Designed by James Renwick and opened in 1879, it is one of the finest Gothic-style structures in America and of course the seat of the Archdiocese of New York. Based on Cologne Cathedral, it is almost as impressive. When it was first built, St Patrick's was outside the city limits. Now it is dwarfed by buildings in the busiest shopping area of town. (Incidentally the first St Patrick's Cathedral, downtown on the corner of Mott and Prince Streets, dates from 1809 and has recently been restored.)

Since Fifth Avenue is New York's main central artery, it is used for every major city parade. One of the most colourful is the **St Patrick's Day Parade** itself (inset right) when the line down the middle of the road is painted green and every leprechaun is out in force.

Among the other noteworthy city churches is

Roberta di Camerino

Riverside Church on Riverside Drive at 122nd Street, also known for its fine Gothic detail. Its 122-metre (400-foot) tower houses the Laura Spelman Rockefeller carillon which has 74 bells. The Church of the Transfiguration on East 29th Street, better known as 'The Little Church Around the Corner', is so pretty it is included on sightseeing tours. Some of its stained glass windows are memorials to famous actors who have worshipped there. Stained glass along with impressive stone carving are some of the exceptional features of the Cathedral of St John the Divine on Amsterdam Avenue and 112th Street.

One of the most unusual buildings to be found in New York is **The Cloisters** (right) in its country setting in Fort Tryon Park. If it looks as if some of medieval Europe has been transported to a clifftop overlooking the Hudson, that's exactly what happened.

Actually, The Cloisters is the medieval department of the Metropolitan Museum of Art. To establish it, a 12th century charter house was brought over intact from Europe, along with four cloisters from monasteries in southern France, parts of a Romanesque church and a 12th century Spanish apse. There are smaller treasures relocated here as well, including rare tapestries like the 15th century 'Hunt of the Unicorn', paintings, frescoes and stained glass. What makes a visit memorable is the peace and quiet – such a change from the rest of Manhattan's noise. Not all of New York's architecture is as glamorous. Tenement buildings with iron fire escape stairways down the front proliferate the upper Manhattan reaches of Harlem and **Spanish Harlem** (below). But they're home to countless Cubans and Puerto Ricans like the children pictured (overleaf).

NEW YORKERS

The New Yorker may live in a four-floor walkup or a luxurious 24-hour, camera-scanned penthouse. Or he may commute from a place across the river where the garden is green and not the tarmaced roof variety. Some New Yorkers sling hash or hawk pretzels for a living; others make million-dollar decisions inside glass cages. Some make eye contact in a singles bar or like to be seen in the trendiest new discothèque; a few create masterpieces in a SoHo loft. The New Yorker is always curious, gregarious – and fickle. At a moment's notice, he may forsake the health club for the covered tennis centre; jogging for roller skates. But he is devoted to his potholed, misunderstood, stimulating city.

Find a native New Yorker and you've found yourself a rare animal. Many of their parents or grandparents will have been born thousands of miles away from Manhattan, for the rush of early immigrants from impoverished parts of Europe has resulted in several strong ethnic areas where the customs and cuisine of the old country have got transplanted to this, the new. Downtown 'Little Italy' is a place of street festivals, while Chinatown's community have pagoda-decorated phone boxes. Up in Germantown, around 86th Street, there are brass bands, beer fests and plenty of apfelstrudel. New Yorkers may be Jewish, Greek, Lebanese or South American too. Wherever there's action, there are the people.

So finding a native New Yorker is not an easy task, but the fact that Manhattan has become a melting pot of many different nationalities is one of the reasons for its air of excitement. New York speaks foreign languages and cooks foreign foods. It sells every product ever made from all over the world. It dances to the bouzouki and the balalaika, snaps the castanets and sings a fado. It is a city of neighbourhoods, created by the hordes of immigrants who sought fresh dreams of a rich life in the New World and chose New York City to fulfil them. For visitors this can mean a home from home.

One of the best ethnic areas for food and fun is Germantown on the Upper East Side, situated in a district called Yorkville. (There is a York Avenue right next to the East River but this extends to exclusive 'millionaires row', Sutton Place in the 50s.) The main street of Germantown is 86th Street, a cross-town road where the traffic travels in both directions. (On minor streets, it goes one way only, usually towards the East River if the number is even, and towards the West when the number is odd.)

Don't be surprised to hear many different languages, for Middle Europeans have established a home from home here. There are restaurants, pastry shops, cinemas showing German films and delicatessens selling sausages. The hofbrauhauses are like those in Bavaria complete with sauerbraten and pretzels, traditional drinking songs and **big horn bands** (above right). In these noisy surroundings there is no shortage of *gemütlichkeit* atmosphere.

Asia chose its stronghold downtown. Well over 6,000

Chinese Americans are packed into the tiny winding alleys and streets of **Chinatown** (below) which begins just below Canal Street on the Lower East Side. It is one of the most exotic city neighbourhoods (albeit crowded especially at weekends with the invasion of Chinese relatives and friends who live elsewhere). Chinatown is a favourite place for a cheap authentic meal. The won ton soup and sweet and sour pork are nearly as reasonable and certainly as good as they are in Hong Kong and the uninitiated can learn how to use chopsticks into the bargain. Shop signs and street banners are in Chinese while Chinatown's telephone kiosks boast decorative pagoda tops. Enough people speak English, however, so there is no language problem in stores or restaurants.

Anyone who has never been to the Far East will marvel at the unusual foods on sale in the grocery and greengrocer shops: 1,000-year-old eggs, dried fish and herbs like ginseng. Rattan work, incense and other Orientalia make good gifts and will probably cost less here than in the midtown shops.

The Chinese celebrate a host of festivals and the Chinese American community is no exception. Chinese New Year, in particular (generally around early February), is celebrated with much enthusiasm. Dragon dances, street parades and fireworks are all features of the festivities at this time of year. The Moon Cake Festival is another fanciful Chinese celebration. Look out for these sweetmeats in Chinatown's shops and buy some to taste. They are made from sugared bean paste and lotus seeds.

Chinatown's main street is Mott and here the Chinese Museum is well worth visiting. A unique collection, even for New York, it depicts 5,000 years of Chinese culture. There are some interesting exhibits on display including a huge Chinese imperial dragon, musical instruments, a replica of a Chinese market, and a Buddhist altar.

New York's large Jewish community is scattered throughout the city and its neighbouring boroughs these days, but it once flourished in the Lower East Side. The first group of Jews came as early as 1654, but it was the mass stream of Jews arriving from Eastern Europe between 1881 and the start of World War 1 who settled down around Orchard Street. At one point, there were as many as one and a half million Jews in this part of town.

Even today, the city houses some two million Jews, which is more than any other country except Israel and Russia, but most of them do not live in Lower East Side tenements. Pedlars and pushcarts are still there, of course, offering secondhand clothes or fresh vegetables, kosher pickles and black bread, but they've been joined by Negroes, Puerto Ricans, Chinese and Italian vendors. Nevertheless a trip to Essex Market and down Orchard Street is still rewarding for its ethnic colour. Like London's Petticoat Lane, the shops in varying sizes are stocked with Jewish books and religious articles along with just about anything else you can name.

In the same vicinity, Henry Street Settlement was founded by Lilian Wald, a Jewish pioneer in social work, and a browse along lower Second Avenue will show what is left of the Jewish theatres. The remains of America's first Jewish cemetery can be found at Chatham Square in the same area. Naturally this section is dotted with yeshivas and synagogues, but the most awe-inspiring synagogue is not in the Lower East Side at all. Temple Emanu-El is located on Fifth Avenue and 65th Street and is the city's largest Jewish house of worship. The Jewish Museum also has an uptown location – at Fifth Avenue and 92nd Street. Displays here include some of the finest collections of Jewish ritual and ceremonial art in the world. Orthodox Jews like the Chasidics tend to live outside Manhattan. For example, many different sects have made parts of **Brooklyn** (above right) their home. One such village where they can lead their cloistered lives undisturbed is New Square. Along Bedford Avenue in Williamsburg, a number of the kaftaned sect go about their business, while Borough Park is almost totally inhabited by Chasidic Jews, as is Crown Heights.

Chances are the **black New Yorker** (below right) lives in Harlem, a district located to the north of Central Park between 110th and 155th Streets. This 9 sq km (3½ square mile) area has seen good times, when its clubs were fun places for the social elite, and bad, when racial conflict caused fires and looting. In the 1920s and 30s everyone who was anyone wanted to go to the 125th Street vicinity speakeasies like the Cotton Club and the Savoy Ballroom where the drinks were cold and the music, hot. The Lafayette Theatre was a famous music hall and Bill 'Bojangles' Robinson named a tree at 131st Street and Seventh Avenue, the tree of hope.

Today most visitors would think twice before entering a Harlem bar. The quarter is rundown and overcrowded, and that tree of hope is only a stump. But hope does prevail. A plaque marks the site and a clever young black team organizes informative sightseeing tours for overseas visitors.

Little Italy (far right) is equally crowded but in the nicest possible way. Italians are volatile yet happy go lucky They love festivals and make delicious pasta.

And all that can be found in the lusty neighbourhood a subway stop or two below Greenwich Village. They seize any opportunity to celebrate a saint's day festooning churches, shrines and buildings with tinsel and ribbons; dancing in the streets and generally making whoopee as only the Italians can. The street markets along Mulberry Street with their garlicky sausage and mozzarella cheese are rich with the flavour of Naples, while the restaurants here and along Broome or Mott Streets probably offer some of the city's best Italian cuisine. Chinatown may have encroached on parts of this Italian territory, but it is still possible to sit with an expresso at a pavement café and pretend you are in the Via Veneto.

For some reason, many Italian Americans join New York's **police force** (left). America's 'cops' are quite a breed. These rough, tough, gun-toting law enforcers couldn't be less like British bobbies, but then they are often confronted by rough tough problems. With such a high density population crammed into a relatively small space, it is not surprising that the crime rate is reasonably high. First-time visitors to New York tend to press their fingers to their ears to lessen the sound of the sirens as police cars hurtle towards the scene of an incident. You can be sure that, at the first sign of trouble, they are on the spot in double-quick time. The cops may not always have a good public image, but they can be friendly and they're certainly human.

Another nationality who seem to be attracted to the police ranks or fire fighting forces is the Irish, who form a very large city contingency. Not all the poor Irish who turned up at New York's docks became millionaires like Alexander T. Stewart, but a goodly number have done well for themselves, for example the famous Kennedy family.

As for those **firemen** (above), they have to be quick off the mark to prevent raging fires destroying buildings in such close proximity of each other. One of the most famous firehouses was at 104 Duane Street. Now the Fire Department Museum, it includes fire fighting equipment such as fire-engines, horse-drawn vehicles and ladder trucks, plus photographs and trophies.

Whatever his ethnic background, the New Yorker is a special person, often harassed, often frenzied, often mixed up, but always curious and outgoing as well. Whatever he works at, he works hard. New York has always been the place to get somewhere. Look at Cornelius Vanderbilt, who began his career as a Staten Island ferryman and was already worth $11 million in 1853 through the operation of steamship services on the Hudson and Long Island Sound.

The New Yorker has always believed he could rise to fame – in the field of finance, on the stage, in a Madison Avenue advertising agency or in politics. A mayor perhaps. Today's mayor lives in Gracie Mansion. The best view of it is from a Circle Line sightseeing cruise which begins at the foot of West 43rd Street and takes about three hours to orbit the island. It is also the easiest way to look at the George Washington Bridge which spans the Hudson at 179th Street, and Grant's Tomb at Riverside Drive and 122nd Street. This granite structure contains the sarcophagi of America's 18th president and his wife, battle flags and memorial resolutions. The boat trip gives a dramatic perspective.

Whatever he does for a living, the New Yorker is bound to be a commuter. He may take the subway which is used by more than three million people a day. (Anyone can ride anywhere on its 461-stop network for a fixed price fare.) He may use the PATH rail rapid transit system from Newark, New Jersey, to the World Trade Center, which like the subway operates around the clock. He may take an express bus from New Jersey into the Port Authority Building on Eighth Avenue, or drive in from the Bronx across the Expressway. He may take a train from Long Island into Penn Station, an extremely busy focal point for midtown – or into Grand Central Station. He may even take a cable car from nearby Roosevelt Island.

If he is a city dweller, the New Yorker may travel on one of the city buses which charge a fixed fare for any given route. Bus stops are found on alternate street corners, travelling up or down town on alternate avenues depending on traffic direction, and going two ways on major crosstown streets such as 14th, 23rd, 34th 42nd and 57th. (Maps of all the ways to get around Manhattan are available at the New York City Convention and Visitors Bureau.) Altogether, the island is linked with New York's other boroughs by four tunnels, eight connecting bridges, seven outlying bridges and a number of parkways and expressways.

However much the New Yorker may groan about work, he can be surprisingly ingenious about getting there. During a citywide transport strike, he has been known to skateboard or roller skate to work and, when the occasional blizzard brings four-wheeled movement to a halt, he'll get out his **skis** (right) and *langlauf* his way to the office!

The favourite meal for a New Yorker may be anything from classical French cuisine in an intimate townhouse to a sizzling steak in a cosy pub, for food is taken quite seriously in New York. There are a host of ethnic choices including exotic soul food or South American. Pick one of the numerous coffee shops for a meal, as they all serve hot dishes as well as snacks, and many have liquor licences for those in the mood for more than a milk shake. As for American sandwiches, they are a far cry from the thin English cucumber and paste variety. A meal in themselves, they come 'over-stuffed' with chicken, tuna fish, pâté and bacon – in fact with dozens of interesting combinations, all garnished with potato chips, pickles and salad. Follow them with a slice of cheesecake, New York style, rich and creamy, guaranteed to be fattening!

If time is particularly short or budget really low, scores of sidewalk kitchens will grill hamburgers or franks on the spot and roast chestnuts in winter. **Street vendors** (inset right) sell pretzels, bagels, cold drinks, ice cream or even froghurt (frozen yoghurt on a stick). These food stands and the self-service chain restaurants with established names are the best bet for a swift snack or a cheap lunch. Every New Yorker knows, for example, that Chock Full O'Nuts still makes some of the best coffee in town, that Horn and Hardart invented the automat and that Tad's started the microwave cooking craze. Nowadays, new fast food chains have followed suit, with Brewburgers, crêperies and French soup kitchens.

Since there are no strict licensing laws, whenever New Yorkers fancy a glass of wine or frothy cocktail,

they are free to indulge; at what is called colloquially a 'Singles Bar' perhaps. There are several good ones in the 60s along First and Second Avenues where chatting up or being chatted up is the name of the game, but which, too, provide good lunches and disco music. At the 'Happy Hour' (a New York invention) cocktails are half price. Usually, this is a feature between 4 pm and 6 pm or 5 pm and 7 pm and free *hors d'oeuvres* are offered as well.

At the weekend, New Yorkers combine breakfast and lunch in one meal after a late morning start to the day. 'Brunch' is served in a variety of establishments on Saturdays and Sundays from around noon until 3 pm. The setting could be somewhere swish with a panoramic view or a friendly, glassed-in pavement café in a residential neighbourhood. For a fixed price they serve eggs benedict or French toast or the more traditional bacon and eggs, thrown in with as many bloody marys, screwdrivers (vodka and orange) or champagne as you can manage.

It is possible to save money by looking out for chain restaurants featuring free wine or beer with a meal, all the salad or as much steak, fish, chicken as you can eat.

America, of course, instigated the world's craving for good basic food served quickly and, of all the fast foods, hamburgers and hot dogs have become international favourites. Even so, the best is still found in New York. **Nathan's hot dogs** (far right) are especially famous. For years, hot dog addicts had to traipse to the large

boardwalk mecca at Brooklyn's Coney Island until Nathan's opened a couple of outlets in the city.

One of the biggest hot dog fans is the New York **cabbie** (above and inset) and a character you can't miss; after all, there are more than 11,000 yellow cabs in the city. It is more than likely that the cabbie will be clutching a cigar, hail from the Bronx or Brooklyn and be ready to talk about anything. Frequently he will moan about the inexpertise of other road users, especially the cyclists, but the latter are something he will have to put up with for cycling is the New Yorker's hobby. It's a cheap way to commute and a healthy one to keep the figure trim. On a Sunday, **bike groups** (right) pedal hell for leather to Central Park where they'll stop for a breather. If it seems as if New Yorkers are always on a health kick, it's because they are. Cycling is not the only hobby that appeals to city dwellers. The park also sees plenty of roller-skaters and joggers, now that both sports are established national pastimes. And after enthusiasm for health clubs waned, the energetic turned to the covered city tennis courts.

Another popular city sport is basketball. All the best college and pro basketball teams (like the Knicks for whom New York is home ground) play at Madison Square Garden, the giant entertainment/sports complex towering above Penn Station on Seventh Avenue. The less famous (and completely unknown) use any of the small courts that dot Manhattan to practise (overleaf).

ENJOYING
THE BIG APPLE

At night when lighted windows in tall blocks wink and blink, New York becomes a glitterland. With its blaze of neon, Broadway comes into its own and suddenly you discover why 42nd Street has always been called 'The Milky Way'. Inside the world's largest theatre, Radio City Music Hall, the Rockettes do their high kicks. Inside an intimate supper club a singer captures an audience with a song. That's entertainment – and Manhattan has lots of it. There are plush nightclubs, fancy discothèques, panoramic cocktail lounges, Irish pubs and quiet piano bars. Something for everyone.

Whatever's 'in' is on – in New York, the city that loves to entertain and be entertained. A night at the Lincoln Center, where foremost ballet and opera companies perform, may call for formal attire, while jeans and sweatshirts are popular gear for watching a boxing match or rock concert at Madison Square Garden. Fans of the avant garde can take themselves off to an off-Broadway or off-off-Broadway production. Art lovers may browse through the Frick or take tea at the Met.

Outside glass enclosed pavement cafés the world wanders by. Inside, strawberry daiquiris add a rosy tinge to the day. Greenwich Village artists offer charcoal sketches for a few dollars but the coffee houses allow you to play chess for free. In Central Park, rowing boats drift on the lake. In vest pocket parks, drifters relax.

Good legs and developed muscles may be a must for sports like basketball, but a different style of good legs are needed to appear at Radio City Music Hall on Sixth Avenue. The **Rockettes** (right) are America's most famous chorus girls who have become world renowned. They are a well-trained *corps de ballet* whose high kicks are in precise unison and whose costumes are as spectacular as those expected of a top nightclub. However, Radio City is a nightclub with a difference. It is not only the world's largest theatre, capable of holding over 6,000 people, but it is also one of the last holdouts from the 1930s and 40s when it was taken for granted that a theatre would offer both film and stage shows for one low price. The newly renovated Radio City is possibly the ultimate in art deco with its black mirrored lounge and curving staircase, and everything presented here is suitable for the entire family. Although there is advance booking, a large number of seats are available on a first come first served basis at the box office.

Not very far away is the most notorious and celebrated New York nightlife centre where Broadway meets 42nd Street. **Times Square** (far right) is in the heart of the theatre district although 'Broadway' is a collective term for more than 35 theatres on Manhattan's West Side in an area that actually extends from 41st to 53rd Streets. Tickets to Broadway shows don't come cheaply but savings can be made by going to a matinee or buying 'twofers'. When a show gets near the end of its run, the house may not be completely full and so often two tickets are sold for the price of one. Twofers are often stacked on shop counters, hotel desks and also the theatre ticket kiosk at Times Square itself.

Music has always been a New York love and, at 1 Broadway, the Songwriters Hall of Fame has memorabilia including George Gershwin's desk, Fats Waller's piano and Duke Ellington's old grand. Other mementoes include old sheet music, manuscripts, player pianos and guitars. Which goes to prove that entertainment isn't just limited to the Times Square area. Indeed, in addition to Village theatre, a dramatic

theatre renaissance has taken place in Chelsea, New York's thriving West Side community where young families are refurbishing brownstones.

The famous 42nd Street was called 'The Milky Way' because at night its multitude of neon-lit cinemas gave a blaze of light. Sadly today most of the movies are pornographic, but New York is hoping to revive 42nd Street's heyday image which will be helped now the new Hyatt hotel has opened. However, nightlife in The Big Apple can be found everywhere; lavish shows in top clubs, smart supper clubs, or hotel nightspots where big names appear. Jazz in particular is back in favour despite a lean period for some years. Now the revival is so strong that jazz clubs are liberally sprinkled throughout the city and there is a jazzline to call to find out who's playing where. Enthusiasts can test their knowledge of the subject by visiting the Jazz Museum at 125 W 55th Street, which tells of the history of jazz through exhibits including posters, paintings, photos, tapes and instruments. From September to June, free concerts are held here.

Folk music can often be found in Village clubs and coffee houses like the more offbeat entertainment – yoga or poetry readings perhaps. These and similar are advertised in *The Village Voice*, a local community newspaper. Ethnic nightspots might include the 'Belly Belt', West Side in the 30s. Here at Middle East and Greek tavernas belly dancing and shish kebabs are the order of the night. There are also showcases for amateur talent, a host of pubs ideal for 'a crawl' and discothèques which rise in favour one year and fall the next. They're all part of New York after dark.

Music and dancing of all kinds can be found but the most splendid and cultured place to appreciate them is at the **Lincoln Center** (above). When it opened, some people were appalled by the design of this complex, while others thought it was the best thing to have happened to New York. The buildings comprise the Metropolitan Opera House, New York State Theater, Vivian Beaumont Theater, Avery Fisher Hall, Alice Tully Hall and Juilliard School – all of which may be toured by day if the inclination to attend an evening performance is lacking. The Lincoln Center is the home of the brilliant New York City Ballet and the Philharmonic Orchestra. The Library and Museum of the Performing Arts here is also involved in the music scene – showcases for young artists are held several times a year in the auditorium. In addition, the New York Shakespeare Festival presents a season at the Center. Art itself is quite visible in the grounds and lobbies, albeit controversial – Alexander Calder's *Le Guichet* in front of the Library, for example; Henry Moore's *Reclining figure* in the reflecting pool near the Beaumont Theater; and Richard Lippold's *Orpheus and Apollo* in the Avery Fisher Hall.

Music, indeed entertainment, of a different kind can be discovered for free in Central Park, New York's biggest recreational area – a great public playground in the midst of stone and cement. **Amateur jugglers** (left) amuse the crowds or a magician suddenly starts his act. An impromptu concert is a frequent occurrence, if only at the whim of some guitar strummers to get an audience to listen or join in. There may be a peace rally in Sheep Meadow or some strange festival, the cause of which is unknown to all save the participants, in full swing under the trees. A handmade necklace or leather purse may be on offer and, who knows, bands of artists may be working on a mile-long painting! Anything goes in Central Park, especially on a Sunday.

All the city's joggers come to exercise in the park and those who are good riders hire a horse and trot through the miles of bridle paths. But probably one of the most pleasant ways to take advantage of Central Park is to see it by **horse-drawn carriage** (below). You can pick one up, plain or fancily decorated with flowers and bells, at 59th Street and Central Park South, near the Plaza Hotel. Generally, they charge by the hour to clip through the park, but sometimes they may be

enticed to take to Fifth Avenue. A carriage ride, even in winter, is a delight and a warm one – they'll draw up the hood and provide blankets.

The park also has a skating rink, adventure playgrounds for youngsters, a zoo and an adjacent children's zoo which proves a treat for tiny tots. Toy boats bob on the pond and kites fly. Adults can enjoy a free summer Shakespeare play, take their own picnic, and people-watch with the rest of the throng around the park's focal point, Bethesda Fountain – or buy from the book stalls and international food stands.

Conservatory Lake (right) at 72nd Street proves to be an unexpected rural spot for New York and one of its most romantic when relaxing in a rowing boat.

Boating uptown is quite different from that downtown. Shipping has always been important to the port of New York. In the old days, the tall ships – giant clippers – came from all over the world to drop anchor at South Street. Times changed and many of the old seamen's stores in the area made way for much-needed office space, but not very long ago a preservation order was put on the streets around Fulton to create the **South Street Seaport Museum** (below). Today, this encompasses what remains of the 19th-century port. In essence, it is a living museum whose streets, old brick counting houses and saloons, narrow alleys and warehouses are relics of earlier days. Some eleven blocks have been reclaimed from neglect, so that New Yorkers and visitors alike can learn about the commercial origins of America and its connection with the sea. It was because of its easy access to the ocean that New York became a great city in the first place.

Today's Fulton Street was a major thoroughfare when the Fulton Ferry started operating in 1816. In 1822, the Fulton Market was established – it is now a fish market – and, when the Erie Canal opened in 1825, all kinds of goods poured into New York's harbour. South Street became known as 'The Street of Ships'.

Today at Piers 15 and 16 you can see the *Peking*, a four-masted German barque built in 1911 which was later renamed the *Arethusa* when she became one of the last square-riggers to be used for commercial purposes. Also preserved are the original Ambrose Lightship and the *Lettie G. Howard*, a Gloucester fishing schooner of the 1890s, plus the *Maj. Gen. William H. Hart*, the last existing Fulton ferry. Visitors can sail aboard the *Pioneer*, a 95-year-old schooner, for a three-hour trip around the harbour; take a very early morning tour of Fulton Street Fish Market; or listen to lectures on maritime topics, finishing at the Museum's shops.

Along with Mom and apple pie, there is nothing more American than baseball. It was probably Babe Ruth who established the sport permanently as a national pastime – and he did it in New York. His home ground was the **Yankee Stadium** (preceding pages) which since its remodelling is one of the world's most modern sports facilities and is nicknamed 'The House that Ruth Built'. Just over 54,000 seats here have an uninterrupted view of the playing fields and some of the assets include a 172-metre (565-foot) electronic score board and instant replay screen. Another popular sport in the United States is American football, and the local New York side is **the Jets** (preceding pages, inset). It is a rough, tough game, requiring padding and helmets. On the other hand, soccer has been gaining in importance recently. New York is certainly a sports capital. Thoroughbreds race all year, and pro ice hockey, basketball, baseball, soccer, pro football all overlap and run into each other, so that spectator sports are easy to attend.

Although really good stretches of sand are few and far between, New York City does have several beaches on its doorstep. Rockaway in Queens, for example, runs for almost 16 kilometres (10 miles) along the shore of the Atlantic Ocean. Jones Beach is perhaps the best of the nearest – wide, white and backed by grassy dunes. It's a Long Island State Park so it's well landscaped and provides all kinds of holiday facilities. But I daresay the most famous – and popular – is **Coney Island** (left). Here New Yorkers can swim and sunbathe (if they can find a patch of unoccupied sand) on a hot summer's day and the amusements, hot dogs and toffee apples will keep the children happy.

All the borough parks offer sports fans things to do. In Pelham Bay's 857 hectares (2,118 acres), for instance, a riding academy, golf, tennis *and* a cricket pitch can be found. Also in The Bronx, Van Cortlandt Park has boating, riding, golfing and tennis, while Brooklyn's Prospect Park includes a zoo, boating lakes and a skating rink. Flushing Meadow Park was once a swamp and was developed in the 1930s to accommodate New York's World Fair. In addition to a marina, there's bicycling, indoor ice skating and a swimming pool. Staten Island's Clove Lake Park boasts riding, boating, fishing, ice skating and a model yacht pond. And at Sheepshead Bay in Brooklyn, party fishing boats depart for an Atlantic trip in search of bluefish or flounder.

MAKING A BUCK

The racks of clothes wheeled down Seventh Avenue will keep you on your toes! Business is brisk in the Garment District and those trolleys move fast, perhaps to ensure an order is filled for Macy's, Manhattan's merchandise mecca. Watch out, too, for anyone with a tagged lapel in the lobbies of the large hotels. Conference delegates love to convene in New York where the atmosphere's right for trading knowledge and ideas, not to mention money.

Trade is a 24-hour Manhattan exercise – from high-level discussions at a Madison Avenue advertising agency to the selling of diamonds at Tiffany's, Fifth Avenue's celebrated jewellery store, for New York is a marketplace and always has been. Currency has been its concern since it started off as a fur trading post – unlike other colonies which were settled as havens for political or religious freedom. With the opening of the Erie Canal, the city became America's leading business centre and, after the American Civil War, international commerce was attracted by its deep-water harbour.

Lower Manhattan still breathes big business. Residential New York may have moved uptown but that money citadel Wall Street stayed down, along with the Stock Exchange and the Federal Reserve Bank. There's big time trade in giant office complexes like the World Trade Center – and small time trade as well: at the Fulton Street fish market and the nearest hamburger stand!

A quick glance at the number of banks and finance houses together with the towering buildings dealing with world marketing, all clustered together at the **downtown tip of Manhattan** (preceding pages), and anyone can see that New York is a key business centre. However, various sections of town tend to specialize in different kinds of business.

If you're looking for exceptional jewellery, take yourself off to Fifth Avenue and **Tiffany's** (right). Even if you're not, this is a marvellous store to browse through. It has always been a famous place for fine jewels but it was made internationally celebrated when the film *Breakfast at Tiffany's* was made, based on a story by Truman Capote and starring Audrey Hepburn. Most of the fine crystal, china and gems are on the ultra expensive side, but there is an excellent gift floor where small sterling silver items can be bought quite cheaply. Like all New York's prestigious stores, Tiffany's giftwraps everything. No flinging into brown paper bags here! Anything, even as tiny as a thimble, is first put in a pale blue felt pouch and then placed in the distinctive Tiffany's pale blue box to be tied with white ribbon. (At Christmas, the box colour changes to red.)

A second great jewellery store is Cartier but, if you'd like to get into the heart of the jewellery scene, stroll through the diamond centre in and around 47th Street and Sixth Avenue. In the myriad of marts, diamonds are traded, polished and retailed. Shopping in New York is always fun. Since the stores don't stick rigidly to January or July for sales, knocked down goods are available somewhere on a year round basis. But beware of those stores (especially in Fifth Avenue) proclaiming they're going out of business – everything 20 per cent or 50 per cent off. They've been going out of business for years!

One of Manhattan's greatest department stores is **Macy's** (right). It claims to be the world's largest store, which is probably true since it not only takes up a block of Seventh Avenue from 34th to 35th Streets, but extends across the Sixth Avenue (Herald Square) as well. Within its ten sales floors it is possible to find literally anything your heart desires whether it's a necessity or merely whimsical.

Adjacent to Macy's is another big department store called Gimbel's, whose basement is a favourite spot for bargain hunters. Ohrbach's on 34th Street, just off Fifth Avenue, features high fashion at low prices. Discontinued designs or slightly irregular garments often find their way to the pegs here to be snapped up by discriminating purchasers. Another budgeteer's paradise is Alexander's on 5th Street and Lexington Avenue (with branches all around New York). This is a good place for linens and records.

Fashionable stores for prestige purchases include Altman's and Lord & Taylor's, both on Fifth, and top of the list, Saks Fifth Avenue, is now into its second half century, still a strong name for elegance. Sometimes, whole stores are devoted to a special theme. Christmas windows are justifiably some of the best in the world, making creative use of mechanized dolls, puppets and

toys. It must be pointed out that New Yorkers adore labels and therefore like to shop at Henri Bendel's and Bonwit's, but they're most affectionate about Bloomingdale's at 59th Street and Lexington. Chic, young (and not so young) sophisticates refer to it as 'Bloomies'. Its scented air and progressive room settings have helped make it a store leader. Now its 'shops within a shop' idea is very popular.

Along Seventh Avenue in the 30s is known as the **Garment District** (right). Here there are a number of wholesale fashion houses as New York is one of the major rag trade centres. From early morning onwards, coaster-wheel racks of clothing are on the move and trucks are loading and unloading merchandise. Casual sportswear in man-made fibres are particularly good buys because Americans make them in a wide range of sizes, including half sizes, for all shapes and heights, from five foot nothing to extra tall, from standard figure

to extra large. Colour and patterns are available, too, in great variety.

The Lower East Side markets and the Village boutiques can quite often produce something original or worthwhile as fads usually start in New York. Remember the button craze, a badge for every occasion, or messages on T-shirts? They're still going strong and now even crazier. The best antiques are generally to be found along with pricey art galleries on upper Madison Avenue, although downtown Second and Third Avenues have managed to retain a few of their junk shops which used to be so abundant. Paper, believe it or not, is a good buy. Who else but Americans would use paper for everything including bikinis? Actually plastic-coated bathroom and picnic wares are very pretty and extremely reasonable, while giftwrapping paper is cheaper and more varied than in Britain.

When New Yorkers refer to 'the five and dime', they usually mean Woolworth's. Most shoppers will be hard put to find anything that only costs a nickle or 10 cents these days, but what they can do is to take a look at the Woolworth Building at 233 Broadway. It has been called 'The Cathedral of Commerce'. The carved spires, richly decorated lobby, three-storey entrance arcade framing a wall of golden veined marble quarried in the Greek isle of Skyros, will serve to show that when those nickles and dimes are added up they make an awful lot of dollars. Wide marble staircases lead to ornately decorated second-floor balconies with their frescoes of

Not surprisingly, **Wall Street** (left) is one of New York's most historic areas. There was once a proper wall here, made from tree trunks by the Dutch settlers to protect them from the then wilderness outside. A good place to start exploration is in the comparative calm of Trinity Church at Broadway and Wall. It is gracefully gothic and former parishioners like Robert Fulton (who has a nearby street named after him) and Alexander Hamilton, are buried in its graveyard.

Stop at the corner of Wall and Nassau Streets for a look at the Federal Hall National Memorial. It was here that John Peter Zenger won his trial to ensure the freedom of the press and George Washington took his oath of office as the first president in 1789. (His statue commemorates the occasion.) The first American congress also assembled here and adopted the Bill of Rights. Nowadays, crowds of office workers throng on its steps to enjoy the sun or listen to a lunchtime concert. The current building was built in 1842 and was originally a customs house, then a sub-treasury and is now a museum – a fine example of Greek Revival architecture.

At Number 23 Wall Street, the headquarters of the J. Pierpont Morgan empire, there are still visible scars of an anarchist's bomb that exploded here in 1920. The ground floor of Citibank's office at 55 Wall Street was built in 1836 as the Merchants Exchange and later served as a customs house being only subsequently remodelled for Citibank use when a second tier was added. Those interested in architecture will note that it is a subtle blend of Ionian and Corinthian styles. Number 74 Wall Street was erected in 1926 for the Seamen's Bank for Savings, the city's second oldest bank and today still a bank, although not necessarily for the seafaring fraternity. When completed it was proclaimed the finest building of its year but the original street address of 76 was changed when seamen pointed out the two numbers added up to 13 – not a good omen! On the site of Number 82, the Tontine Building, stood the Tontine Coffee House (1792) which was where a band of 18th-century militants helped plan the American Revolution.

Big Business happens, as well, at Liberty Street. Number 33 is the site of the Federal Reserve Bank of New York, a renaissance palace full of money. This is where the banks bank and where foreign governments loan and repay each other simply by moving gold bars from one vault to another. You can tour the vaults and other departments but reservations must be made in advance.

That may be the old empire but the brand new commercial complex is the **World Trade Center** (right). The earth and rock excavated to make way for was placed in the Hudson River to create new land which is currently being developed as Battery Park City. Built by the Port Authority of New York and New Jersey and opened in 1973, the World Trade Center was planned to provide the port with new headquarters for the transaction of international business.

More than 900 firms and organizations are presently operating out of the Center. Tenants include importers, exporters, freight forwarders and banks. Altogether, some 50,000 office workers earn their living here, supplemented by 80,000 visiting businessmen and tourists. At the moment, four exchanges share the

Commerce and *Labor*. The vaulted ceiling is set with brilliantly coloured glass mosaics, and the wrought iron cornices are gold-leafed.

Everyone knows that the amusing carved figures under the crossbeams in the lobby arcade of the first floor portray Frank Woolworth, Cass Gilbert the architect, Louis Horowitz the builder, Lewis Pierson the building's first tenant and president of the Irving Bank, renting agent Edward Hogan and engineer Gunwald Aus. Each is shown doing something associated with their work – counting those coins in Woolworth's case!

Money! And oh how that money changes hands quickly, albeit on paper down at the **Stock Exchange** (preceding pages). When the first stock exchange was set up under a buttonwood tree in 1792, it was rather different to the one you can see today on the corner of Broad and Wall Streets. You can't miss it, built as it is in 'renaissance temple' style. Inside, stockbrokers act for clients from all over the world, buying and selling millions of dollars worth of securities in minutes. Inside it might well seem that all hell is breaking loose, but of course the gesticulating men know what they're doing. For visitors interested in learning more, a guided tour is offered frequently between Monday and Friday, and a film is shown in the exhibit hall. Otherwise, just watching from the Visitors' Gallery can be instructive.

Center's huge trading floor: The Commodity Exchange; The New York Coffee, Sugar and Cocoa Exchange; The New York Cotton Exchange; and the New York Mercantile Exchange. The activity that goes on at this level seems violent and argumentative, but it is merely the way general transactions are carried on. It is possible to watch from the Visitors' Gallery or a party of five can book in advance for a guided explanatory tour.

When you realize that the Center's plaza is equivalent in size to four football fields, you can begin to see how large it actually is. The towers rise 412 metres (1,350

feet) and each one has 100 lifts including a direct one to the top. The observation deck is on the 107th floor of the South Tower with an open air platform on the 110th – and it remains open until fairly late in the evening. An alternative would be to have a drink or meal in the bar and restaurant, Windows on the World. The ground floor (known as a concourse in Americanese) boasts a diverse number of restaurants from fast food operations to something a bit more luxurious, plus all kinds of shops to wander around.

As mentioned earlier, shipping was a major aspect of

business life in downtown Manhattan. However, with the development of modern handling methods, this is no longer the case, and cargo now goes through container terminals in Brooklyn, Staten Island and, most important of all, Port Elizabeth in New Jersey. The small bursts of melancholy sound likely to be heard in Manhattan during the twilight hours will almost certainly stem from the river. **Tug boats** (below) patrol the waters or perhaps announce the arrival or departure of some larger ship. Gone are the days when great liners lined up the canyon of Broadway with the Chrysler Building

to be certain they were in the right channel. Not many cruise ships call these days and Cunard Lines headquarters (almost as big as Penn Station) is now a post office, while the company resides in midtown. The Customs House no longer stands on old 'Shipping Row' and today many of the piers on the West Side are decaying relics of a bygone era.

However, Manhattan is still used by passenger liners like the *QE2*, and such operations are handled by the new terminal on the Hudson River between 48th and 52nd Streets. This modern, 40 million dollar complex has lounges for passengers and parking spaces for 1,000 cars.

Downtown commerce used to include many things. It was in this part of town that Manhattan got its first lights when Thomas Edison perfected his electric lamp in 1879. He settled on 225 Pearl Street for his first central commercial generating station. It served an area of about 2·5 sq km (1 sq mile) known as the 'First District'. Also, part of downtown was known as Newspaper Row. During the early 1890s, in the area around Spruce Street, 19 daily papers were printed in New York along with even more foreign language ones. Hanover Square, now a park, was the city's original printing-house square near which William Bradford established the colony's first printing press in 1693. Today, most of the newspapers have closed or moved uptown although the old Sun Building still stands. The *New York Times* used to be published at Number 41 Park Row until 1904 when it changed location. New sites can still be landmarks like today's *Daily News* Building on East 42nd Street, which has been a milestone of modern

architecture since 1930. It is noted for its great revolving globe in the lobby.

Edison's lights have been used for a lot more than just lighting the downtown quarter. They light up bill board advertising which is now a trademark of New York. The most famous ad of this type is the one overlooking **Times Square** (above left). Most usually it is used to advertise cigarettes such as Winston but sometimes it will portray an iron. What makes this billboard so famous is the puff of smoke that is emitted every so often making it ideal for cigarette or steam iron display. Whether or not one uses the product, it is an advertisement which has long fascinated both New Yorkers and out-of-towners.

Much of the cargo which used to find its way to New York's port – exotic spices, herbs, strange fruits – continues to arrive only more quickly. Products from every country may be found in New York. In some instances, as with Japan, representation may mean a modern showcase shop. In other cases, it's a **street vendor's cart** (above right) which displays pistachio and other nuts from Greece or elsewhere.

America's own products are often on view at the Exhibition Center at Columbus Circle when international buyers attend trade shows. Even more businessmen are expected when Manhattan's new convention centre is built.

Million dollar decisions are made in super glossy buildings along **Park Avenue** (right) and perhaps this view from the Pan Am Building sums up New York. In the busy canyons of the metropolis, day to day life is carried on at Big Apple pace. And that's fast!

Index

Page numbers in italics refer to illustrations

Alice Tulley Hall 45
Allied Chemicals Exhibit Center 23
Avery Fisher Hall 45

Battery, The *2–3*; Battery Park 10;
  Battery Park City 58
Bentley Manor House 10
Borough Park, Brooklyn 32
Bowling Green 10
Broadway 10, 15, 42, 61
Bronx 20, 51
Brooklyn 15, *32*, 51, 61
Brooklyn Bridge 10, *12–13*, *14*, 15
Burlington Industries 'The Mill' 23

Castle Clinton 10, 15
Central Park *4–5*, *6*, 7, 32, 38, 42, *44*, 45–6, *47*
Chelsea 42
Chinatown 7, 30, 31, *31*, 35
Chinese Museum 31
Chrysler Building 20, *21*, 61
Church of the Transfiguration 26
Citibank Office 58
Citicorp Center 20
City Hall 15; City Hall Park 15
Cloisters, The 26, *27*
Clove Lake Park 51
Coney Island 38, *50*, 51
Conservatory Lake 46, *47*
Contemporary Crafts Museum 24
Customs House 10, 62

Daily News Building 62

Eastman Kodak photo centre 23
Ellis Island 10
Empire State Building *18*, 20, 23
Essex Market 32
Exhibition Center, Columbus Circle 62

Federal Hall National Memorial 58
Federal Reserve Bank of New York 58
Fifth Avenue 20, 24, *25*, 32, 54
Fire Department Museum 35
Flushing Meadow Park 51
Forest Hills 20
Fort Tryon Park 26, *27*
Fort Wadsworth 10
42nd Street 42
Fraunces Tavern 15, *15*
Frick Collection 24, 42
Fulton Street 15, 46, 51, 54

Garment District 54, *55*
George Washington Bridge 35
Germantown 7, 30, *30*
Governor's Island 10
Gracie Mansion 35
Grand Central Station 23, 36
Grant's Tomb 35
Greenwich Village *17*, 17, 35, 42, 55
Guggenheim Museum 10, 24, *24*

Hanover Square 62
Harlem 7, 26, 32
Henry Street Settlement 32
Hyatt Hotel 42

Jazz Museum 42
Jewish Museum 32
Jones Beach 51
Juilliard School 45

Lafayette Theatre 32
Lever House 23
Liberty Island 10, *11*
Lincoln Center 42, 45, *45*
Little Italy 7, 30, 32, *33*, 35
Lower East Side 31, 32, 55

MacDougal Street 17
McGraw Hill Building 20
Macy's 54, *55*
Madison Square Garden 38, 42
Manhattan *2–3*, *8–9*, 10, *12–13*, 15, 17, *18–19*, 20, 24, 26, 30, 36, 42, *52–3*, 62
Methodist Church, Old John Street 15
Metropolitan Museum of Art 24, 26, 42
Metropolitan Opera House 45
Milton Steinberg Building 23
Museum of Modern Art 24

Nathan's hot dogs 38, *39*
New Square 32
New York State Theater 45

Pan Am Building *22*, 23, 62
Park Avenue *22*, 23, 62, *63*
Pelham Bay 51
Performing Arts, Library and Museum of 45
Port Elizabeth, New Jersey 61
Prospect Park 51
Provincetown Playhouse 17

Queens 20, 51

RCA Building 20
Radio City Music Hall 20, 42, *42*
Richmondtown 10
Riverside Church 26
Rockaway Beach 51
Rockefeller Center 20, *20*

St John the Divine, Cathedral of 26
St John's Church 15
St Patrick's Cathedral 20, 24, *25*
St Paul's Chapel 15
Seagram Building 23
Seamen's Bank for Savings 58
Shea Stadium 20
Sheepshead Bay 51
Snug Harbor 10
SoHo *16*, 17
Songwriters Hall of Fame 42
South Street Seaport Museum 46, *46*
Spanish Harlem 26, *28–29*
Staten Island 10, 15, 51, 61
Statue of Liberty 10, *11*
Stock Exchange *56–7*, 58

Temple Emanu-El 32
Tiffany's 54, *54*
Times Square 23, 42, *43*, 62, 62
Tontine Building 58
Trinity Church 10, 15, 58

Union Carbide Building 23
United Nations Building 23, *23*

Van Cortlandt Park 51
Verrazano-Narrows Bridge 7, 15
Vivian Beaumont Theater 45

Waldorf Astoria Hotel 23
Wall Street 10, 54, 58, *58*
Washington Square 10, 17
Whitney Museum 10, 24
Woolworth Building 10, 55, 58
World Trade Center *1*, 10, 15, 20, 54, 58, *59*

Yankee Stadium *48–9*, 51

Acknowledgements

The publishers would like to thank the following organizations and individuals for their kind permission to reproduce the photographs in this book:

Barbara Burns/Image Bank 37 inset; Pat Canova/Image Bank 15; Alan Choisnet/Image Bank 26 left; Ian Cobb/Image Bank 50–51; Richard Cooke 11, 21, 48–49, 49 inset, 62 left; Ian Dawson 30 above, 46 below; Greg Evans 18, 20; Lawrence Fried/Image Bank 34, 57 inset; Mitchell Funk/Image Bank 59; Bob Gelberg/Image Bank 2–3; Alfred Gescheidt/Image Bank 38 inset 60–61; Melchior di Giacomo/Image Bank 8 9, 19; Geoffrey Gove/Image Bank 16, 17; S. Green-Armytage/Image Bank 45; Tim Holt/Image Bank 35; Angelo Hornak 24; Image Bank 40–41; L.H. Javitz/Image Bank 58; Whitney Lane/Image Bank 26–27; Larry Lee/Image Bank 11 inset; Harvey Lloyd/Image Bank 16 inset; Jay Maisel/Image Bank 63; Peter Miller/Image Bank 4–5; B. Mitchell/Image Bank 42, 56–57; Roy Morsch/Image Bank 36–37; J. Barry O'Rourke/Image Bank 55 below; Spectrum Colour Library 46 above, 55 above; Richard Steedman/Image Bank 12–13, 44–45, 47; Charles Steiner/Image Bank 43; Tiffany & Co. 54; Georges Tourdjman/Image Bank 39 above right; Mireille Vautier/De Nanxe 1, 14, 23, 25, 28–29, 30–31, 32, 38–39 above, 52–53, 62 right; Luis Villota/Image Bank 22, 25 inset; George Wright 6–7, 33, 39 below.

PDO 82-0360